50 Korean BBQ Recipes for Home

By: Kelly Johnson

Table of Contents

- Classic Bulgogi (Marinated Grilled Beef)
- Galbi (Grilled Short Ribs)
- Samgyeopsal (Grilled Pork Belly)
- Dak Bulgogi (Marinated Grilled Chicken)
- Bulgogi Nachos
- Kimchi Fried Rice
- Spicy Pork Bulgogi
- LA Galbi (Flanken-Style Short Ribs)
- Grilled Mackerel (Godeungeo Gui)
- Korean BBQ Tofu Skewers
- Spicy Chicken Skewers (Dak Kkochi)
- Kalbi Chim (Braised Short Ribs)
- Spicy Grilled Shrimp
- Beef Bulgogi Lettuce Wraps
- Grilled Vegetable Bibimbap
- Japchae (Stir-Fried Glass Noodles)
- Kimchi Pancakes (Kimchijeon)
- Grilled Oysters with Gochujang Butter
- Sesame Soy Garlic Marinade for BBQ
- Grilled Squid (Ojingeo Gui)
- Korean BBQ Meatballs
- Spicy Grilled Octopus (Nakji Bokkeum)
- Gochujang Glazed Ribs
- Bulgogi Pizza
- Grilled Korean Corn Cheese
- Kimchi Grilled Cheese Sandwich
- Gochujang BBQ Chicken Wings
- Grilled Tteok (Korean Rice Cakes)
- Dak Gui (Korean Grilled Chicken)
- Bulgogi-stuffed Mushrooms
- Grilled Pork Belly Wraps (Bossam)
- Gochujang Honey Glazed Salmon
- Spicy Grilled Tofu
- Korean BBQ Cauliflower Bites
- Grilled Portobello Mushrooms with Sesame Dressing

- Grilled Sweet Potatoes with Soy Glaze
- Bulgogi Burritos
- Kimchi Quesadillas
- Grilled Miso-Ginger Glazed Eggplant
- Soy Sesame Grilled Scallops
- Gochujang Glazed Brussels Sprouts
- Bulgogi Lettuce Cup Tacos
- Grilled Pineapple with Honey-Soy Glaze
- Bulgogi Sliders
- Spicy Grilled Avocado
- Grilled Korean Egg Toast
- Korean BBQ Meat Skewers
- Bulgogi-stuffed Bell Peppers
- Grilled Kimchi Stuffed Mushrooms
- Korean BBQ Chicken Pizza

Classic Bulgogi (Marinated Grilled Beef)

Ingredients:

- 1.5 to 2 pounds (680-907g) thinly sliced beef (ribeye or sirloin)
- 1 medium-sized onion, thinly sliced
- 3-4 green onions, chopped into 2-inch pieces
- 2 tablespoons sesame oil
- 1 tablespoon toasted sesame seeds (for garnish)

For the Marinade:

- 1/2 cup soy sauce
- 1/4 cup sugar
- 3 tablespoons mirin (rice wine) or cooking wine
- 2 tablespoons honey or corn syrup
- 1 tablespoon grated ginger
- 4 cloves garlic, minced
- 1/4 teaspoon black pepper

Instructions:

In a bowl, whisk together all the marinade ingredients until the sugar is fully dissolved.
Place the thinly sliced beef in a large bowl, and add the sliced onions and chopped green onions.
Pour the marinade over the beef and vegetables. Use your hands or tongs to ensure the beef is thoroughly coated. Marinate for at least 30 minutes to an hour, or refrigerate overnight for more intense flavors.
Heat a grill or grill pan over medium-high heat.
Drizzle sesame oil over the marinated beef and toss to coat.
Grill the beef slices, turning occasionally, until they are cooked to your desired level of doneness and have a nice caramelized exterior.
During the last few minutes of grilling, you can add additional sliced green onions for a fresh touch.
Remove the bulgogi from the grill and transfer it to a serving plate.
Garnish with toasted sesame seeds and additional green onions if desired.
Serve the Classic Bulgogi with steamed rice, in lettuce wraps (ssam), or with your favorite side dishes like kimchi.

Enjoy the deliciously savory and sweet flavors of this Korean BBQ favorite!

Galbi (Grilled Short Ribs)

Ingredients:

- 2 to 3 pounds (907-1361g) beef short ribs, flanken-cut (about 1/3 to 1/2 inch thick)
- 1 medium-sized pear, peeled and grated
- 1 small onion, grated
- 1/2 cup soy sauce
- 3 tablespoons mirin (rice wine) or cooking wine
- 2 tablespoons honey or corn syrup
- 3 tablespoons brown sugar
- 4 cloves garlic, minced
- 1 tablespoon sesame oil
- 1/4 teaspoon black pepper
- 2 green onions, chopped (for garnish)
- Toasted sesame seeds (for garnish)

Instructions:

In a bowl, combine the grated pear, grated onion, soy sauce, mirin, honey, brown sugar, minced garlic, sesame oil, and black pepper. Mix well to create the marinade.
Place the beef short ribs in a large dish or resealable plastic bag.
Pour the marinade over the short ribs, making sure they are evenly coated.
Marinate for at least 2 hours, or preferably overnight in the refrigerator.
Preheat your grill or grill pan to medium-high heat.
Remove the short ribs from the marinade and shake off excess marinade.
Grill the short ribs for about 3-4 minutes on each side, or until they are cooked to your desired level of doneness and have a nice caramelized exterior.
While grilling, baste the ribs with any remaining marinade for added flavor.
Transfer the grilled short ribs to a serving plate.
Garnish with chopped green onions and toasted sesame seeds.
Serve the Galbi hot with steamed rice, in lettuce wraps (ssam), or with other Korean side dishes.

Enjoy the mouthwatering and savory taste of Galbi, a Korean BBQ classic that is sure to be a hit at any gathering!

Samgyeopsal (Grilled Pork Belly)

Ingredients:

- 1 to 1.5 pounds (450-680g) pork belly, thinly sliced
- Fresh lettuce leaves (for wrapping)
- Ssamjang (Korean soybean paste and chili paste)
- Garlic cloves, peeled
- Fresh green chili peppers, sliced
- Sesame oil
- Salt and pepper

Instructions:

Preheat your grill or grill pan over medium-high heat.
Arrange the thinly sliced pork belly on a platter.
Season both sides of the pork belly slices with a pinch of salt and pepper.
Place the pork belly slices on the hot grill and cook for about 2-3 minutes on each side, or until they are cooked through and have a nice char.
While grilling, you can brush the pork belly with a little sesame oil for added flavor.
Remove the grilled pork belly from the heat and transfer to a serving plate.
Serve the Samgyeopsal with fresh lettuce leaves for wrapping.
Accompany the grilled pork belly with Ssamjang (soybean paste and chili paste), peeled garlic cloves, sliced green chili peppers, and a dipping bowl of sesame oil with a pinch of salt and pepper.
To enjoy, place a slice of grilled pork belly on a lettuce leaf, add a small amount of Ssamjang, a garlic clove, and a slice of green chili. Wrap it up and enjoy the delicious combination of flavors.
Repeat the process with various accompaniments, experimenting with different combinations.

Samgyeopsal is a delightful Korean BBQ experience that you can enjoy with family and friends. The interactive nature of wrapping your own pork belly bites in lettuce leaves makes it a fun and social dining experience.

Dak Bulgogi (Marinated Grilled Chicken)

Ingredients:

- 1.5 to 2 pounds (680-907g) boneless, skinless chicken thighs or breasts, thinly sliced
- 1/2 cup soy sauce
- 3 tablespoons mirin (rice wine) or cooking wine
- 2 tablespoons honey or brown sugar
- 2 tablespoons sesame oil
- 4 cloves garlic, minced
- 1 tablespoon grated ginger
- 1 tablespoon gochujang (Korean red chili paste)
- 1 teaspoon black pepper
- 2 green onions, chopped (for garnish)
- Toasted sesame seeds (for garnish)

Instructions:

In a bowl, combine soy sauce, mirin, honey, sesame oil, minced garlic, grated ginger, gochujang, and black pepper. Mix well to create the marinade.
Place the thinly sliced chicken in a large dish or resealable plastic bag.
Pour the marinade over the chicken, making sure it is evenly coated. Marinate for at least 30 minutes to an hour, or refrigerate overnight for enhanced flavors.
Preheat your grill or grill pan to medium-high heat.
Remove the chicken from the marinade and shake off any excess.
Grill the chicken slices for about 3-4 minutes on each side, or until they are cooked through and have a nice char.
While grilling, you can baste the chicken with any remaining marinade for added flavor.
Transfer the grilled chicken to a serving plate.
Garnish with chopped green onions and toasted sesame seeds.
Serve Dak Bulgogi hot with steamed rice or as part of a Korean BBQ spread.

Enjoy the delightful combination of savory, sweet, and slightly spicy flavors in this Dak Bulgogi recipe. It's a perfect dish for a Korean BBQ feast or a quick and flavorful weeknight meal.

Bulgogi Nachos

Ingredients:

For the Bulgogi:

- 1 to 1.5 pounds (450-680g) thinly sliced beef (ribeye or sirloin)
- 1 medium-sized onion, thinly sliced
- 3-4 green onions, chopped into 2-inch pieces
- 2 tablespoons sesame oil

For the Bulgogi Marinade:

- 1/2 cup soy sauce
- 1/4 cup sugar
- 3 tablespoons mirin (rice wine) or cooking wine
- 2 tablespoons honey or corn syrup
- 1 tablespoon grated ginger
- 4 cloves garlic, minced
- 1/4 teaspoon black pepper

For the Nachos:

- Tortilla chips
- Shredded cheese (cheddar or a blend of Mexican cheeses)
- Jalapeños, sliced
- Sour cream
- Guacamole or diced avocados
- Fresh cilantro, chopped
- Sesame seeds (for garnish)

Instructions:

In a bowl, whisk together all the bulgogi marinade ingredients until the sugar is fully dissolved.

Place the thinly sliced beef in a large dish or resealable plastic bag. Add the sliced onions and chopped green onions.

Pour the bulgogi marinade over the beef and vegetables. Use your hands or tongs to ensure the beef is thoroughly coated. Marinate for at least 30 minutes to an hour, or refrigerate overnight for more intense flavors.

Heat a skillet or pan over medium-high heat. Add sesame oil and cook the marinated bulgogi until it is fully cooked and has a nice caramelized exterior. Remove from heat.

Preheat your oven to broil.

Arrange tortilla chips on a baking sheet.

Top the tortilla chips with the cooked bulgogi, spreading it evenly.

Sprinkle shredded cheese over the bulgogi-topped chips.

Place the baking sheet under the broiler for 2-3 minutes, or until the cheese is melted and bubbly.

Remove the Bulgogi Nachos from the oven and add sliced jalapeños, dollops of sour cream, guacamole or diced avocados, and fresh cilantro.

Garnish with sesame seeds for an extra touch.

Serve the Bulgogi Nachos hot as a flavorful and unique appetizer or snack.

Enjoy the delightful fusion of Korean and Mexican flavors in these Bulgogi Nachos, a perfect dish for sharing at gatherings or for a fun and tasty meal at home.

Kimchi Fried Rice

Ingredients:

- 2 cups cooked and cooled rice (preferably day-old)
- 1 cup kimchi, chopped
- 1/2 cup kimchi juice (from the kimchi jar)
- 1 cup cooked protein (such as diced tofu, shredded cooked chicken, or thinly sliced beef)
- 2 tablespoons vegetable oil
- 1 onion, finely chopped
- 2 cloves garlic, minced
- 1 carrot, finely diced
- 2 green onions, sliced
- 2 tablespoons soy sauce
- 1 tablespoon sesame oil
- 1 teaspoon sugar (optional)
- 1/2 teaspoon black pepper
- Sesame seeds, for garnish
- Fried eggs (optional, for serving)

Instructions:

Heat vegetable oil in a large skillet or wok over medium-high heat.
Add chopped onions and minced garlic. Stir-fry for 1-2 minutes until the onions are translucent and the garlic is fragrant.
Add diced carrots to the skillet and continue to stir-fry for another 2-3 minutes until the carrots are slightly softened.
Add chopped kimchi to the skillet and stir-fry for an additional 2-3 minutes.
Add the cooked protein of your choice (tofu, chicken, or beef) to the skillet. Stir to combine with the other ingredients.
Add the cooked and cooled rice to the skillet. Break up any clumps and mix well with the other ingredients.
Pour in the kimchi juice and soy sauce. Stir-fry the rice mixture for 3-4 minutes until everything is well combined and heated through.
Drizzle sesame oil over the fried rice and sprinkle sugar (if using) and black pepper. Toss to coat evenly.
Add sliced green onions and continue to stir-fry for another minute.

Taste the fried rice and adjust the seasoning if needed, adding more soy sauce or sesame oil according to your preference.

Remove the skillet from heat. Garnish the Kimchi Fried Rice with sesame seeds. Optionally, serve the fried rice with a fried egg on top for an extra layer of flavor and richness.

Serve the Kimchi Fried Rice hot, either as a standalone dish or as a side.

Enjoy the robust and tangy flavors of Kimchi Fried Rice, a comforting and satisfying dish that brings together the goodness of kimchi and perfectly cooked rice.

Spicy Pork Bulgogi

Ingredients:

- 1 to 1.5 pounds (450-680g) thinly sliced pork belly or pork shoulder
- 1/2 cup gochujang (Korean red chili paste)
- 1/4 cup soy sauce
- 3 tablespoons mirin (rice wine) or cooking wine
- 2 tablespoons honey or brown sugar
- 2 tablespoons sesame oil
- 4 cloves garlic, minced
- 1 tablespoon grated ginger
- 1 teaspoon black pepper
- 1 tablespoon vegetable oil (for cooking)
- 2 green onions, chopped (for garnish)
- Toasted sesame seeds (for garnish)

Instructions:

In a bowl, combine gochujang, soy sauce, mirin, honey, sesame oil, minced garlic, grated ginger, and black pepper. Mix well to create the marinade.
Place the thinly sliced pork in a large dish or resealable plastic bag.
Pour the spicy marinade over the pork, making sure it is evenly coated. Marinate for at least 30 minutes to an hour, or refrigerate overnight for more intense flavors.
Heat vegetable oil in a large skillet or wok over medium-high heat.
Remove the pork from the marinade and shake off any excess.
Add the marinated pork to the hot skillet and stir-fry for 5-7 minutes, or until the pork is fully cooked and has a nice caramelized exterior.
During the last few minutes of cooking, you can add chopped green onions and toss to combine.
Transfer the Spicy Pork Bulgogi to a serving plate.
Garnish with additional chopped green onions and toasted sesame seeds.
Serve the Spicy Pork Bulgogi hot with steamed rice or as part of a Korean BBQ spread.

Enjoy the bold and fiery flavors of Spicy Pork Bulgogi, a delightful Korean dish that's sure to satisfy your cravings for spicy and savory goodness.

LA Galbi (Flanken-Style Short Ribs)

Ingredients:

- 2 to 3 pounds (907-1361g) beef short ribs, flanken-cut (about 1/3 to 1/2 inch thick)
- 1 cup soy sauce
- 1/2 cup brown sugar
- 1/4 cup mirin (rice wine) or cooking wine
- 1/4 cup sesame oil
- 4 cloves garlic, minced
- 1 tablespoon grated ginger
- 1 tablespoon honey
- 1 teaspoon black pepper
- 2 green onions, chopped (for garnish)
- Toasted sesame seeds (for garnish)

Instructions:

In a bowl, combine soy sauce, brown sugar, mirin, sesame oil, minced garlic, grated ginger, honey, and black pepper. Mix well to create the marinade.
Place the flanken-cut beef short ribs in a large dish or resealable plastic bag.
Pour the marinade over the short ribs, making sure they are evenly coated.
Marinate for at least 2 hours, or preferably overnight in the refrigerator.
Preheat your grill or grill pan to medium-high heat.
Remove the short ribs from the marinade and shake off any excess.
Grill the short ribs for about 3-4 minutes on each side, or until they are cooked through and have a nice char.
While grilling, you can baste the ribs with any remaining marinade for added flavor.
Transfer the grilled LA Galbi to a serving plate.
Garnish with chopped green onions and toasted sesame seeds.
Serve the LA Galbi hot with steamed rice or as part of a Korean BBQ spread.

Enjoy the succulent and flavorful LA Galbi, a classic Korean BBQ dish that showcases the delicious taste of marinated and grilled beef short ribs.

Grilled Mackerel (Godeungeo Gui)

Ingredients:

- 2 to 4 mackerel fillets
- 2 tablespoons soy sauce
- 1 tablespoon mirin (rice wine) or cooking wine
- 1 tablespoon sesame oil
- 1 tablespoon honey or brown sugar
- 1 tablespoon minced garlic
- 1 teaspoon grated ginger
- 1 tablespoon vegetable oil (for brushing on the grill)
- Sesame seeds (for garnish)
- Sliced green onions (for garnish)

Instructions:

In a bowl, whisk together soy sauce, mirin, sesame oil, honey or brown sugar, minced garlic, and grated ginger to create the marinade.
Place the mackerel fillets in a shallow dish or resealable plastic bag.
Pour the marinade over the mackerel fillets, ensuring they are well coated.
Marinate for at least 30 minutes, allowing the flavors to penetrate the fish.
Preheat your grill or grill pan to medium-high heat. Brush the grill grates with vegetable oil to prevent sticking.
Remove the mackerel from the marinade, shaking off any excess.
Grill the mackerel fillets for approximately 3-4 minutes on each side, or until the fish is fully cooked and has nice grill marks.
While grilling, you can baste the fillets with additional marinade for added flavor.
Transfer the grilled mackerel to a serving plate.
Garnish with sesame seeds and sliced green onions.
Serve the Grilled Mackerel hot with steamed rice and your favorite side dishes.

Enjoy the distinct and savory flavor of Godeungeo Gui, a delightful Korean dish that's not only tasty but also rich in omega-3 fatty acids found in mackerel.

Korean BBQ Tofu Skewers

Ingredients:

For the Tofu Marinade:

- 1 block (14-16 ounces) firm or extra-firm tofu, pressed and cubed
- 3 tablespoons soy sauce
- 1 tablespoon mirin (rice wine) or cooking wine
- 1 tablespoon sesame oil
- 1 tablespoon brown sugar
- 2 cloves garlic, minced
- 1 teaspoon grated ginger
- 1 tablespoon vegetable oil (for grilling)

For the Skewers:

- Wooden or metal skewers, soaked in water if using wooden ones
- Vegetables of your choice (bell peppers, cherry tomatoes, mushrooms, onions, zucchini, etc.)

For Garnish:

- Toasted sesame seeds
- Chopped green onions
- Sesame oil for drizzling

Instructions:

In a bowl, whisk together soy sauce, mirin, sesame oil, brown sugar, minced garlic, and grated ginger to create the marinade.
Press the tofu to remove excess water, then cut it into bite-sized cubes.
Place the tofu cubes in the marinade, ensuring they are well-coated. Allow the tofu to marinate for at least 30 minutes, or longer for more flavor.
Preheat your grill or grill pan over medium-high heat.
Thread marinated tofu cubes and your choice of vegetables onto the skewers.
Brush the skewers with vegetable oil to prevent sticking.

Grill the skewers for about 3-4 minutes on each side, or until the tofu and vegetables have a nice char and are cooked through.

While grilling, you can baste the skewers with any remaining marinade for added flavor.

Once the skewers are cooked, remove them from the grill and transfer to a serving plate.

Garnish the Korean BBQ Tofu Skewers with toasted sesame seeds and chopped green onions.

Drizzle a little sesame oil over the skewers for extra richness.

Serve the skewers hot as a delightful and flavorful vegetarian or vegan option for Korean BBQ.

These Korean BBQ Tofu Skewers are not only delicious but also versatile, allowing you to customize the vegetables to your liking. Enjoy the savory and aromatic flavors with a touch of smokiness from the grill.

Spicy Chicken Skewers (Dak Kkochi)

Ingredients:

For the Chicken Marinade:

- 1.5 to 2 pounds (680-907g) boneless, skinless chicken thighs or breasts, cut into bite-sized pieces
- 1/4 cup soy sauce
- 2 tablespoons gochugaru (Korean red chili powder)
- 2 tablespoons gochujang (Korean red chili paste)
- 2 tablespoons honey or brown sugar
- 2 tablespoons mirin (rice wine) or cooking wine
- 2 tablespoons sesame oil
- 3 cloves garlic, minced
- 1 tablespoon grated ginger
- 1 tablespoon vegetable oil (for grilling)

For the Skewers:

- Wooden or metal skewers, soaked in water if using wooden ones

For Garnish:

- Chopped green onions
- Sesame seeds

Instructions:

In a bowl, whisk together soy sauce, gochugaru, gochujang, honey or brown sugar, mirin, sesame oil, minced garlic, and grated ginger to create the marinade. Cut the chicken into bite-sized pieces and place them in the marinade. Toss to ensure the chicken is well-coated. Marinate for at least 30 minutes, or refrigerate for a few hours for more intense flavors.
Preheat your grill or grill pan over medium-high heat.
Thread the marinated chicken pieces onto the skewers.
Brush the skewers with vegetable oil to prevent sticking.

Grill the skewers for about 3-4 minutes on each side, or until the chicken is fully cooked and has a nice char.

While grilling, you can baste the skewers with any remaining marinade for added flavor.

Once the skewers are cooked, remove them from the grill and transfer to a serving plate.

Garnish the Spicy Chicken Skewers with chopped green onions and sesame seeds.

Serve the Dak Kkochi hot as a delightful and slightly spicy appetizer or part of a Korean BBQ spread.

Enjoy the bold and spicy flavors of these Dak Kkochi skewers, a fantastic addition to your grilling repertoire!

Kalbi Chim (Braised Short Ribs)

Ingredients:

- 2 to 3 pounds (907-1361g) beef short ribs, cut crosswise into 2-inch pieces
- 1 large onion, sliced
- 3 carrots, peeled and cut into chunks
- 1 cup shiitake mushrooms, sliced
- 4 cloves garlic, minced
- 1 tablespoon vegetable oil
- 4 cups beef broth
- 1/2 cup soy sauce
- 1/4 cup mirin (rice wine) or cooking wine
- 2 tablespoons sugar
- 1 tablespoon sesame oil
- 1 teaspoon black pepper
- 1 tablespoon toasted sesame seeds (for garnish)
- Sliced green onions (for garnish)

Instructions:

In a large pot or Dutch oven, heat vegetable oil over medium-high heat.
Sear the beef short ribs on all sides until browned. Remove the ribs from the pot and set them aside.
In the same pot, add sliced onions and minced garlic. Saute until the onions are softened.
Add the seared short ribs back to the pot.
Pour in the beef broth, soy sauce, mirin, sugar, sesame oil, and black pepper. Stir to combine.
Bring the mixture to a boil, then reduce the heat to low. Cover the pot and simmer for about 1.5 to 2 hours, or until the beef is tender.
Add the carrots and shiitake mushrooms to the pot. Continue to simmer for an additional 30-45 minutes until the vegetables are cooked and the beef is fork-tender.
Adjust the seasoning if needed, adding more soy sauce or sugar according to your taste.
Once the Kalbi Chim is ready, transfer it to a serving platter.
Garnish with toasted sesame seeds and sliced green onions.

Serve the Braised Short Ribs hot over steamed rice or alongside other Korean side dishes.

Enjoy the rich and savory flavors of Kalbi Chim, a comforting and hearty Korean dish that's perfect for a family meal or special occasion.

Spicy Grilled Shrimp

Ingredients:

- 1 pound large shrimp, peeled and deveined
- 2 tablespoons olive oil
- 3 cloves garlic, minced
- 1 teaspoon paprika
- 1 teaspoon cayenne pepper (adjust to your spice preference)
- 1 teaspoon smoked paprika
- 1 teaspoon dried oregano
- 1 teaspoon ground cumin
- 1 teaspoon brown sugar
- 1/2 teaspoon salt
- 1/4 teaspoon black pepper
- Zest and juice of 1 lime
- Wooden or metal skewers (if using wooden, soak them in water for 30 minutes)

Instructions:

In a bowl, combine olive oil, minced garlic, paprika, cayenne pepper, smoked paprika, dried oregano, ground cumin, brown sugar, salt, black pepper, lime zest, and lime juice. Mix well to create the marinade.

Add the peeled and deveined shrimp to the marinade, ensuring they are well-coated. Marinate for about 15-30 minutes.

Preheat your grill or grill pan over medium-high heat.

Thread the marinated shrimp onto skewers.

Grill the shrimp skewers for approximately 2-3 minutes per side or until they are opaque and have nice grill marks.

While grilling, you can baste the shrimp with any remaining marinade for added flavor.

Remove the Spicy Grilled Shrimp from the grill and transfer to a serving plate.

Garnish with chopped fresh cilantro or parsley.

Serve the shrimp hot as an appetizer or main dish. You can also squeeze additional lime juice over the top for a burst of freshness.

Enjoy the kick of spice and the smoky flavor from the grill in these Spicy Grilled Shrimp.

They make a fantastic addition to any barbecue or seafood feast.

Beef Bulgogi Lettuce Wraps

Ingredients:

For the Beef Bulgogi:

- 1 to 1.5 pounds (450-680g) thinly sliced beef (ribeye or sirloin)
- 1 medium-sized onion, thinly sliced
- 3-4 green onions, chopped into 2-inch pieces
- 2 tablespoons sesame oil

For the Bulgogi Marinade:

- 1/2 cup soy sauce
- 1/4 cup sugar
- 3 tablespoons mirin (rice wine) or cooking wine
- 2 tablespoons honey or corn syrup
- 1 tablespoon grated ginger
- 4 cloves garlic, minced
- 1/4 teaspoon black pepper

For the Lettuce Wraps:

- Large lettuce leaves (such as iceberg or butter lettuce)
- Cooked white rice
- Ssamjang (Korean soybean paste and chili paste)
- Garlic cloves, peeled
- Sliced green chili peppers (optional)

Instructions:

In a bowl, whisk together all the Bulgogi marinade ingredients until the sugar is fully dissolved.

Place the thinly sliced beef in a large bowl, and add the sliced onions and chopped green onions.

Pour the Bulgogi marinade over the beef and vegetables. Use your hands or tongs to ensure the beef is thoroughly coated. Marinate for at least 30 minutes to an hour, or refrigerate overnight for more intense flavors.

Heat a skillet or grill pan over medium-high heat.

Drizzle sesame oil over the marinated beef and toss to coat.

Cook the beef slices for about 3-4 minutes on each side, or until they are cooked to your desired level of doneness and have a nice caramelized exterior.
During the last few minutes of cooking, you can add additional sliced green onions for a fresh touch.
Remove the Beef Bulgogi from the heat and transfer it to a serving plate.
To assemble the Lettuce Wraps, take a lettuce leaf, add a spoonful of cooked rice, a few pieces of Beef Bulgogi, and a dollop of Ssamjang.
Add a peeled garlic clove and sliced green chili peppers if desired.
Wrap the lettuce around the filling to create a bite-sized parcel.
Repeat the process with various accompaniments, experimenting with different combinations.

Serve the Beef Bulgogi Lettuce Wraps as a fun and interactive meal, allowing everyone to customize their wraps according to their preferences. Enjoy the vibrant and savory flavors!

Grilled Vegetable Bibimbap

Ingredients:

For the Grilled Vegetables:

- 2 cups shiitake mushrooms, sliced
- 2 cups zucchini, julienned
- 2 cups carrots, julienned
- 2 cups spinach
- 1 cup bean sprouts
- 1 tablespoon vegetable oil
- Salt and pepper to taste

For the Bibimbap Sauce:

- 1/4 cup soy sauce
- 2 tablespoons gochujang (Korean red chili paste)
- 1 tablespoon sesame oil
- 1 tablespoon sugar
- 1 tablespoon rice vinegar
- 2 cloves garlic, minced

For the Bibimbap Bowls:

- Cooked white rice
- Fried eggs (one per serving)
- Sesame seeds (for garnish)
- Sliced green onions (for garnish)
- Kimchi (optional, for serving)

Instructions:

Preheat your grill or grill pan over medium-high heat.
In a bowl, toss the sliced shiitake mushrooms, julienned zucchini, and julienned carrots with vegetable oil. Season with salt and pepper.

Grill the mushrooms, zucchini, and carrots until they are cooked and have nice grill marks. Set aside.

Blanch the spinach in boiling water for about 30 seconds, then immediately transfer to ice water to cool. Squeeze out excess water and season with a bit of salt.

Blanch the bean sprouts in boiling water for about 1-2 minutes. Drain and set aside.

In a small bowl, whisk together the Bibimbap sauce ingredients: soy sauce, gochujang, sesame oil, sugar, rice vinegar, and minced garlic. Adjust the seasoning to your taste.

Assemble the Bibimbap bowls by placing a generous serving of cooked white rice in the center.

Arrange the grilled vegetables, blanched spinach, and bean sprouts around the rice.

Top each bowl with a fried egg.

Drizzle the Bibimbap sauce over the vegetables and rice.

Garnish with sesame seeds and sliced green onions.

Serve the Grilled Vegetable Bibimbap hot, with kimchi on the side if desired.

Mix the ingredients together before eating to enjoy the combination of flavors and textures. Grilled Vegetable Bibimbap is a vibrant and satisfying dish that provides a wonderful balance of colors, flavors, and nutrition.

Japchae (Stir-Fried Glass Noodles)

Ingredients:

- 200g (7 ounces) Korean sweet potato starch noodles (dangmyeon)
- 1/2 cup thinly sliced beef (ribeye or sirloin)
- 1 medium-sized carrot, julienned
- 1 red bell pepper, julienned
- 1 yellow bell pepper, julienned
- 1 onion, thinly sliced
- 2 cups spinach, blanched and squeezed dry
- 2-3 shiitake mushrooms, sliced
- 2 tablespoons vegetable oil (for cooking)
- 2 cloves garlic, minced
- 2 tablespoons soy sauce
- 1 tablespoon sugar
- 1 tablespoon sesame oil
- Toasted sesame seeds (for garnish)
- Sliced green onions (for garnish)

Instructions:

Cook the sweet potato starch noodles (dangmyeon) according to the package instructions. Drain and rinse them under cold water. Cut the noodles with scissors into shorter, more manageable lengths.
In a bowl, marinate the thinly sliced beef with soy sauce, sugar, and minced garlic. Set aside for about 15-20 minutes.
Heat a large skillet or wok over medium-high heat. Add 1 tablespoon of vegetable oil.
Stir-fry the marinated beef until it is fully cooked. Remove it from the skillet and set aside.
In the same skillet, add another tablespoon of vegetable oil.
Stir-fry the sliced onion until it becomes translucent.
Add the julienned carrot, red bell pepper, yellow bell pepper, and shiitake mushrooms. Continue to stir-fry until the vegetables are tender.
Add the blanched spinach and cooked beef back into the skillet. Mix well.
Add the cooked sweet potato starch noodles to the vegetables and meat. Pour soy sauce and sesame oil over the noodles.

Stir-fry everything together until well combined and heated through.
Taste and adjust the seasoning if needed, adding more soy sauce or sugar according to your preference.
Transfer the Japchae to a serving platter and garnish with toasted sesame seeds and sliced green onions.
Serve the Japchae hot or at room temperature as a delicious and colorful Korean noodle dish.

Japchae is a versatile and satisfying dish that can be enjoyed as a main course or a side dish. Its sweet and savory flavors, combined with the chewy texture of the glass noodles, make it a favorite among many.

Kimchi Pancakes (Kimchijeon)

Ingredients:

- 1 cup kimchi, finely chopped
- 1 cup all-purpose flour
- 1/2 cup water
- 1 egg
- 1 tablespoon soy sauce
- 1 tablespoon sesame oil
- 2 green onions, finely chopped
- 1/4 cup kimchi juice (liquid from the kimchi jar)
- Vegetable oil for frying

Dipping Sauce:

- 2 tablespoons soy sauce
- 1 tablespoon rice vinegar
- 1 teaspoon sesame oil
- 1 teaspoon sesame seeds
- 1 green onion, finely chopped (optional)

Instructions:

In a large mixing bowl, combine the chopped kimchi, flour, water, egg, soy sauce, sesame oil, and chopped green onions. Mix well until a batter forms.
Add kimchi juice to the batter and stir to combine. The batter should be thick but pourable.
Heat a non-stick skillet or frying pan over medium heat. Add a generous amount of vegetable oil to coat the bottom of the pan.
Once the oil is hot, spoon a portion of the batter into the pan, spreading it out to form a pancake. You can make small or large pancakes, depending on your preference.
Cook the pancake for 2-3 minutes on each side, or until golden brown and crispy.
Repeat the process with the remaining batter, adding more oil to the pan as needed.
For the dipping sauce, mix together soy sauce, rice vinegar, sesame oil, sesame seeds, and chopped green onions.
Serve the Kimchi Pancakes hot with the dipping sauce on the side.

Enjoy these flavorful and crispy Kimchi Pancakes as a delightful Korean appetizer or snack. They are perfect for sharing and pair well with the tangy dipping sauce.

Grilled Oysters with Gochujang Butter

Ingredients:

- 12 fresh oysters, shucked
- 1/2 cup unsalted butter, softened
- 2 tablespoons gochujang (Korean red chili paste)
- 2 cloves garlic, minced
- 1 tablespoon soy sauce
- 1 tablespoon honey or brown sugar
- 1 tablespoon rice vinegar
- Chopped green onions for garnish
- Lime wedges for serving

Instructions:

Preheat your grill to medium-high heat.
In a bowl, mix together the softened butter, gochujang, minced garlic, soy sauce, honey or brown sugar, and rice vinegar. Stir until well combined.
Arrange the shucked oysters on a grill-safe tray or plate.
Place a small dollop of the gochujang butter mixture on top of each oyster.
Carefully place the tray on the preheated grill and close the lid. Grill for about 5-7 minutes or until the oysters are cooked and the edges start to curl.
While grilling, you can baste the oysters with some additional gochujang butter for extra flavor.
Remove the grilled oysters from the grill and transfer them to a serving plate. Garnish with chopped green onions.
Serve the Grilled Oysters with Gochujang Butter hot, accompanied by lime wedges for squeezing over the top.

Enjoy the unique combination of flavors in these Grilled Oysters with Gochujang Butter – the spicy, sweet, and savory glaze adds a delicious twist to the classic grilled oyster experience.

Sesame Soy Garlic Marinade for BBQ

Ingredients:

- 1/4 cup soy sauce
- 2 tablespoons sesame oil
- 2 tablespoons honey or brown sugar
- 3 cloves garlic, minced
- 1 tablespoon rice vinegar
- 1 tablespoon fresh ginger, grated
- 1 tablespoon toasted sesame seeds
- 2 green onions, finely chopped
- 1/4 teaspoon black pepper

Instructions:

In a bowl, whisk together soy sauce, sesame oil, honey or brown sugar, minced garlic, rice vinegar, grated ginger, toasted sesame seeds, chopped green onions, and black pepper.

Taste the marinade and adjust the sweetness or saltiness according to your preference by adding more honey or soy sauce.

Use the marinade immediately or refrigerate for at least 30 minutes to allow the flavors to meld.

Place your choice of protein (chicken, beef, pork, tofu, etc.) in a shallow dish or a resealable plastic bag.

Pour the Sesame Soy Garlic Marinade over the protein, ensuring it is well-coated. If using a bag, remove excess air before sealing.

Marinate the protein in the refrigerator for at least 30 minutes, or preferably longer for more intense flavor. Overnight marination is ideal for the best results.

Preheat your grill or barbecue.

Remove the protein from the marinade and grill to your desired level of doneness. While grilling, you can baste the protein with the reserved marinade for extra flavor.

Serve the grilled protein hot, garnished with additional chopped green onions and sesame seeds if desired.

This Sesame Soy Garlic Marinade adds a delightful combination of savory, nutty, and slightly sweet flavors to your grilled dishes. It's perfect for BBQ, adding depth and richness to your favorite proteins.

Grilled Squid (Ojingeo Gui)

Ingredients:

- 2 medium-sized whole squids, cleaned and gutted
- 2 tablespoons soy sauce
- 1 tablespoon gochugaru (Korean red chili flakes)
- 1 tablespoon sesame oil
- 1 tablespoon honey or brown sugar
- 2 cloves garlic, minced
- 1 teaspoon grated ginger
- 1 tablespoon rice wine or mirin
- Sesame seeds and chopped green onions for garnish
- Lime wedges for serving

Instructions:

Prepare the squid by cleaning and gutting them. Score the squid in a crisscross pattern on the inside, being careful not to cut all the way through.
In a bowl, whisk together soy sauce, gochugaru, sesame oil, honey or brown sugar, minced garlic, grated ginger, and rice wine or mirin.
Place the cleaned squids in a shallow dish or resealable plastic bag.
Pour the marinade over the squids, ensuring they are well-coated. Marinate for at least 30 minutes, allowing the flavors to infuse.
Preheat your grill or grill pan over medium-high heat.
Grill the squids for about 3-4 minutes on each side or until they are cooked through and have a nice char.
While grilling, you can baste the squids with any remaining marinade for added flavor.
Transfer the Grilled Squid to a serving plate.
Garnish with sesame seeds and chopped green onions.
Serve the Ojingeo Gui hot, accompanied by lime wedges for squeezing over the top.

Enjoy the succulent and savory taste of Grilled Squid with a hint of heat from the gochugaru. This dish makes a fantastic appetizer or main course, perfect for seafood lovers.

Korean BBQ Meatballs

Ingredients:

For the Meatballs:

- 1 pound ground beef or a mix of beef and pork
- 1/2 cup breadcrumbs
- 1/4 cup milk
- 1/4 cup finely chopped onion
- 1 large egg
- 2 cloves garlic, minced
- 1 tablespoon soy sauce
- Salt and pepper to taste
- Sesame seeds and chopped green onions for garnish (optional)

For the Korean BBQ Sauce:

- 1/4 cup soy sauce
- 2 tablespoons brown sugar
- 1 tablespoon honey
- 1 tablespoon mirin (rice wine) or rice vinegar
- 1 tablespoon sesame oil
- 2 cloves garlic, minced
- 1 teaspoon grated ginger
- 1 tablespoon cornstarch (optional, for thickening)

Instructions:

Preheat your oven to 400°F (200°C).
In a large bowl, combine ground meat, breadcrumbs, milk, chopped onion, egg, minced garlic, soy sauce, salt, and pepper. Mix until well combined.
Shape the mixture into meatballs, approximately 1 to 1.5 inches in diameter, and place them on a baking sheet lined with parchment paper.
Bake the meatballs in the preheated oven for about 15-20 minutes or until they are cooked through and browned on the outside.

While the meatballs are baking, prepare the Korean BBQ sauce. In a saucepan over medium heat, combine soy sauce, brown sugar, honey, mirin, sesame oil, minced garlic, and grated ginger. Bring the mixture to a simmer.
If you prefer a thicker sauce, mix cornstarch with a little water to create a slurry. Stir the slurry into the sauce and simmer until it thickens.
Once the meatballs are cooked, transfer them to a bowl and pour the Korean BBQ sauce over them. Gently toss the meatballs to coat them in the sauce.
Garnish with sesame seeds and chopped green onions if desired.
Serve the Korean BBQ Meatballs hot as an appetizer or main dish. They can be enjoyed on their own or with rice.

These Korean BBQ Meatballs are a crowd-pleaser, offering a perfect balance of savory and sweet flavors with a touch of umami. Enjoy the deliciousness of Korean BBQ in a bite-sized, meatball form!

Spicy Grilled Octopus (Nakji Bokkeum)

Ingredients:

- 1 pound fresh octopus, cleaned and prepared
- 2 tablespoons gochugaru (Korean red chili flakes)
- 2 tablespoons soy sauce
- 1 tablespoon gochujang (Korean red chili paste)
- 1 tablespoon honey or brown sugar
- 1 tablespoon mirin (rice wine) or cooking wine
- 2 tablespoons sesame oil
- 3 cloves garlic, minced
- 1 tablespoon grated ginger
- 1 tablespoon sesame seeds
- Green onions, chopped, for garnish
- Lime wedges for serving

Instructions:

Clean and prepare the fresh octopus. If using frozen octopus, thaw it thoroughly according to the package instructions.
In a bowl, mix together gochugaru, soy sauce, gochujang, honey or brown sugar, mirin, sesame oil, minced garlic, grated ginger, and sesame seeds to create the marinade.
Cut the octopus into bite-sized pieces for easier grilling.
Toss the octopus pieces in the marinade, ensuring they are well-coated. Marinate for at least 30 minutes to allow the flavors to penetrate.
Preheat your grill or grill pan over medium-high heat.
Thread the marinated octopus pieces onto skewers or use a grill basket for easier grilling.
Grill the octopus for about 3-4 minutes on each side or until it is cooked through and has a nice char.
While grilling, you can baste the octopus with any remaining marinade for extra flavor.
Once the octopus is cooked, transfer it to a serving plate.
Garnish with chopped green onions.
Serve the Spicy Grilled Octopus hot, with lime wedges on the side for squeezing over the top.

Enjoy the tender and spicy goodness of Nakji Bokkeum, a delightful Korean grilled octopus dish that makes a fantastic appetizer or main course.

Gochujang Glazed Ribs

Ingredients:

For the Ribs:

- 2 racks of baby back ribs
- Salt and black pepper to taste
- 1 tablespoon vegetable oil

For the Gochujang Glaze:

- 1/4 cup gochujang (Korean red chili paste)
- 1/4 cup soy sauce
- 3 tablespoons honey or brown sugar
- 2 tablespoons rice vinegar
- 2 tablespoons sesame oil
- 3 cloves garlic, minced
- 1 tablespoon grated ginger
- Sesame seeds and chopped green onions for garnish

Instructions:

Preheat your oven to 300°F (150°C).
Prepare the racks of baby back ribs by removing the membrane on the back of the ribs. Season the ribs with salt and black pepper.
Heat vegetable oil in an oven-safe skillet or roasting pan over medium-high heat. Sear the ribs on both sides until they are browned. This step helps to lock in the flavor.
While the ribs are searing, prepare the gochujang glaze. In a bowl, whisk together gochujang, soy sauce, honey or brown sugar, rice vinegar, sesame oil, minced garlic, and grated ginger.
Once the ribs are browned, brush them generously with the gochujang glaze on both sides.
Transfer the skillet or roasting pan to the preheated oven.
Roast the ribs in the oven for 2 to 2.5 hours or until they are tender and cooked through. You can baste the ribs with the glaze every 30 minutes for extra flavor.

During the last 10-15 minutes of cooking, turn on the broiler to caramelize the glaze and give the ribs a nice char.
Once the ribs are cooked, remove them from the oven and let them rest for a few minutes.
Garnish the Gochujang Glazed Ribs with sesame seeds and chopped green onions.
Slice the ribs between the bones and serve them hot.

Enjoy the deliciously sticky and flavorful Gochujang Glazed Ribs as a delightful main dish for your next barbecue or family dinner.

Bulgogi Pizza

Ingredients:

For the Bulgogi:

- 1 pound thinly sliced beef (ribeye or sirloin)
- 1/2 cup soy sauce
- 1/4 cup sugar
- 3 tablespoons mirin (rice wine) or cooking wine
- 2 tablespoons sesame oil
- 3 cloves garlic, minced
- 1 tablespoon grated ginger
- 2 green onions, chopped
- 1 tablespoon vegetable oil (for cooking)

For the Pizza:

- Pizza dough (store-bought or homemade)
- 1 cup shredded mozzarella cheese
- 1 cup sliced bell peppers (assorted colors)
- 1/2 cup sliced red onions
- 1/2 cup sliced mushrooms
- Sesame seeds and chopped green onions for garnish
- Sriracha or gochujang (optional, for extra spice)

Instructions:

For the Bulgogi:

> In a bowl, mix together soy sauce, sugar, mirin, sesame oil, minced garlic, grated ginger, and chopped green onions to create the Bulgogi marinade.
> Add the thinly sliced beef to the marinade, ensuring the meat is well-coated.
> Marinate for at least 30 minutes to allow the flavors to infuse.
> Heat vegetable oil in a skillet or wok over medium-high heat.
> Stir-fry the marinated beef until it is cooked through and has a nice caramelized exterior. Remove from heat and set aside.

For the Pizza:

Preheat your oven to the temperature recommended on the pizza dough package.
Roll out the pizza dough on a floured surface to your desired thickness.
Transfer the rolled-out dough to a pizza stone or baking sheet.
Spread a thin layer of Bulgogi sauce from the cooked beef onto the pizza dough.
Sprinkle shredded mozzarella cheese evenly over the sauce.
Distribute the cooked Bulgogi beef, sliced bell peppers, red onions, and mushrooms on top of the cheese.
Bake the pizza in the preheated oven according to the dough package instructions or until the crust is golden and the cheese is melted and bubbly.
Remove the Bulgogi Pizza from the oven and garnish with sesame seeds and chopped green onions.
If desired, drizzle Sriracha or dollops of gochujang over the pizza for extra spice.
Slice and serve the Bulgogi Pizza hot.

Enjoy the delightful fusion of Korean and Italian flavors in this Bulgogi Pizza, perfect for a unique and delicious meal.

Grilled Korean Corn Cheese

Ingredients:

- 4 ears of corn, husked
- 1 tablespoon vegetable oil
- 1 cup shredded mozzarella cheese
- 1/2 cup shredded cheddar cheese
- 1/2 cup mayonnaise
- 2 tablespoons sweetened condensed milk
- 1 tablespoon unsalted butter
- 1/2 teaspoon garlic powder
- 1/4 teaspoon black pepper
- Chopped green onions for garnish (optional)
- Red pepper flakes for garnish (optional)

Instructions:

Preheat your grill to medium-high heat.
Brush each ear of corn with vegetable oil to prevent sticking.
Grill the corn on the preheated grill, turning occasionally, until the kernels are lightly charred and cooked through. This usually takes about 10-15 minutes.
While the corn is grilling, prepare the cheese mixture. In a bowl, combine mozzarella cheese, cheddar cheese, mayonnaise, sweetened condensed milk, garlic powder, and black pepper. Mix until well combined.
Once the corn is grilled, remove it from the grill.
Cut the kernels off the cobs using a sharp knife.
In a skillet or oven-safe dish, melt the butter over medium heat.
Add the grilled corn kernels to the skillet and sauté for a couple of minutes until they are coated in butter.
Reduce the heat to low and add the cheese mixture to the skillet, stirring to combine with the corn.
Continue cooking and stirring until the cheese is melted and the mixture is well combined.
Optional: If using an oven-safe skillet, you can place it under the broiler for a couple of minutes to achieve a golden and bubbly top.
Garnish with chopped green onions and red pepper flakes if desired.
Serve the Grilled Korean Corn Cheese hot as a side dish or appetizer.

Enjoy the creamy and cheesy goodness of Grilled Korean Corn Cheese with the sweetness of corn and the savory richness of the cheese mixture. It's a delightful treat that pairs well with grilled meats or as a standalone dish.

Kimchi Grilled Cheese Sandwich

Ingredients:

- 4 slices of bread (white, whole wheat, or your preference)
- Butter, softened
- 1 cup shredded cheddar cheese
- 1 cup kimchi, drained and chopped
- 2 green onions, chopped
- 2 tablespoons mayonnaise
- Sriracha or gochujang (optional, for extra spice)

Instructions:

Heat a non-stick skillet or griddle over medium heat.
Butter one side of each slice of bread.
Place two slices of bread, buttered side down, on a clean surface.
In a bowl, mix together the shredded cheddar cheese, chopped kimchi, green onions, and mayonnaise.
Spread the kimchi and cheese mixture evenly on the unbuttered side of the bread slices.
If you like extra spice, you can drizzle Sriracha or spread gochujang on top of the kimchi and cheese mixture.
Top each with the remaining slices of bread, buttered side facing up.
Place the sandwiches in the preheated skillet or griddle.
Grill each side until the bread is golden brown, and the cheese is melted and gooey.
Press down on the sandwiches with a spatula while grilling to ensure even melting.
Once both sides are grilled to perfection, remove the sandwiches from the skillet.
Let them cool for a moment before slicing.
Slice diagonally and serve the Kimchi Grilled Cheese Sandwich hot.

Enjoy the unique and delicious combination of melted cheese, tangy kimchi, and the slight heat from the green onions. The addition of kimchi brings a flavorful twist to the classic grilled cheese sandwich, making it a tasty and satisfying meal.

Gochujang BBQ Chicken Wings

Ingredients:

For the Chicken Wings:

- 2 pounds chicken wings, split into flats and drumettes
- Salt and black pepper to taste
- 1 tablespoon vegetable oil

For the Gochujang BBQ Sauce:

- 1/4 cup gochujang (Korean red chili paste)
- 2 tablespoons soy sauce
- 2 tablespoons honey
- 1 tablespoon rice vinegar
- 1 tablespoon sesame oil
- 2 cloves garlic, minced
- 1 teaspoon grated ginger
- Sesame seeds and chopped green onions for garnish (optional)

Instructions:

Preheat your oven to 425°F (220°C).
Pat the chicken wings dry with paper towels and season with salt and black pepper.
Place the seasoned wings in a large bowl, add vegetable oil, and toss to coat.
Arrange the wings on a baking sheet lined with parchment paper, ensuring they are not too crowded.
Bake in the preheated oven for 45-50 minutes or until the wings are golden brown and crispy, flipping them halfway through.
While the wings are baking, prepare the Gochujang BBQ sauce. In a bowl, whisk together gochujang, soy sauce, honey, rice vinegar, sesame oil, minced garlic, and grated ginger.
Once the wings are cooked, transfer them to a large bowl.
Pour the Gochujang BBQ sauce over the wings and toss until they are evenly coated.

Optional: For extra flavor, you can return the sauced wings to the oven and broil for a few minutes until the sauce caramelizes slightly.
Garnish with sesame seeds and chopped green onions if desired.
Serve the Gochujang BBQ Chicken Wings hot as an appetizer or main course.

Enjoy the deliciously sweet, savory, and spicy flavors of these Gochujang BBQ Chicken Wings. They make a fantastic addition to any gathering or game day feast.

Grilled Tteok (Korean Rice Cakes)

Ingredients:

- 1 pound Korean rice cakes (tteok), sliced into bite-sized pieces
- Water for soaking
- Wooden skewers, soaked in water for at least 30 minutes
- Sesame oil for brushing (optional)
- Brown sugar or honey for drizzling (optional)

Instructions:

Soak the sliced rice cakes in water for at least 30 minutes. This helps to soften them and prevents sticking during grilling.
Preheat your grill to medium-high heat.
Thread the soaked rice cake slices onto the soaked wooden skewers.
Brush the grill grates with a bit of oil to prevent sticking.
Place the skewers on the preheated grill and cook for about 2-3 minutes on each side or until the rice cakes develop grill marks and become slightly crispy on the outside.
Optional: Brush the grilled tteok with sesame oil for extra flavor.
Once the tteok is grilled to your liking, remove the skewers from the grill.
Optional: Drizzle the grilled tteok with brown sugar or honey for a touch of sweetness.
Serve the Grilled Tteok immediately while hot.

Enjoy these Grilled Tteok skewers as a delightful snack or dessert. The grilling adds a smoky flavor and a crispy texture to the rice cakes, making them a unique and tasty treat.

Dak Gui (Korean Grilled Chicken)

Ingredients:

For the Marinade:

- 1.5 to 2 pounds of chicken pieces (thighs, drumsticks, or wings)
- 1/4 cup soy sauce
- 2 tablespoons gochujang (Korean red chili paste)
- 2 tablespoons honey or brown sugar
- 2 tablespoons mirin (rice wine) or cooking wine
- 1 tablespoon sesame oil
- 3 cloves garlic, minced
- 1 tablespoon grated ginger
- 1 tablespoon vegetable oil (for grilling)
- Sesame seeds and chopped green onions for garnish (optional)

Instructions:

In a bowl, whisk together soy sauce, gochujang, honey or brown sugar, mirin, sesame oil, minced garlic, and grated ginger to create the marinade.
Place the chicken pieces in a large bowl or resealable plastic bag.
Pour the marinade over the chicken, making sure each piece is well-coated.
Marinate for at least 30 minutes to allow the flavors to infuse. For a richer flavor, you can marinate the chicken for a few hours or overnight in the refrigerator.
Preheat your grill to medium-high heat.
Remove the chicken from the marinade and let any excess drip off.
Brush the grill grates with vegetable oil to prevent sticking.
Place the chicken pieces on the preheated grill and cook for about 15-20 minutes, turning occasionally, or until the chicken is fully cooked and has a nice char.
Optional: Baste the chicken with any remaining marinade during grilling for extra flavor.
Once the chicken is cooked, transfer it to a serving plate.
Garnish with sesame seeds and chopped green onions if desired.
Serve the Dak Gui hot, either on its own or with steamed rice and your favorite side dishes.

Enjoy the savory and slightly spicy goodness of Korean Grilled Chicken with this Dak Gui recipe. The combination of soy sauce, gochujang, and honey creates a flavorful marinade that elevates the grilled chicken to a delicious and satisfying dish.

Bulgogi-stuffed Mushrooms

Ingredients:

- 12-15 large button mushrooms, cleaned and stems removed
- 1/2 pound thinly sliced beef (ribeye or sirloin)
- 1/4 cup soy sauce
- 2 tablespoons brown sugar
- 1 tablespoon sesame oil
- 2 cloves garlic, minced
- 1 tablespoon grated ginger
- 2 green onions, finely chopped
- 1 tablespoon vegetable oil
- Sesame seeds and chopped green onions for garnish (optional)

Instructions:

Preheat your oven to 375°F (190°C).
Clean the mushrooms and remove the stems. Set the mushroom caps aside.
In a bowl, mix soy sauce, brown sugar, sesame oil, minced garlic, grated ginger, and chopped green onions to create the bulgogi marinade.
Thinly slice the beef and add it to the marinade, ensuring the meat is well-coated. Let it marinate for at least 30 minutes.
Heat vegetable oil in a skillet over medium-high heat.
Cook the marinated beef in the skillet until it is fully cooked and has a nice caramelized exterior. Set aside.
Stuff each mushroom cap with a portion of the cooked bulgogi.
Place the stuffed mushrooms on a baking sheet lined with parchment paper.
Bake in the preheated oven for about 15-20 minutes or until the mushrooms are tender and cooked through.
Optional: Sprinkle sesame seeds and chopped green onions on top for garnish.
Serve the Bulgogi-stuffed Mushrooms hot as an appetizer.

These Bulgogi-stuffed Mushrooms make for a flavorful and elegant appetizer, perfect for gatherings or parties. The combination of the tender beef and savory mushroom caps creates a delightful bite-sized treat with a Korean twist.

Grilled Pork Belly Wraps (Bossam)

Ingredients:

For the Grilled Pork Belly:

- 1 pound pork belly, thinly sliced
- 2 tablespoons soy sauce
- 2 tablespoons mirin (rice wine) or cooking wine
- 1 tablespoon sugar
- 1 tablespoon minced garlic
- 1 tablespoon sesame oil
- Black pepper to taste

For the Wraps:

- Lettuce leaves (such as green leaf or butter lettuce)
- Ssamjang (Korean dipping sauce)
- Kimchi
- Sliced garlic
- Sliced green onions
- Cooked rice (optional)

Instructions:

In a bowl, mix together soy sauce, mirin, sugar, minced garlic, sesame oil, and black pepper to create the marinade.
Place the thinly sliced pork belly in a shallow dish or a resealable plastic bag.
Pour the marinade over the pork belly, ensuring each slice is well-coated.
Marinate for at least 30 minutes, or longer for more flavor.
Preheat your grill or grill pan over medium-high heat.
Grill the marinated pork belly slices for about 2-3 minutes on each side or until they are cooked through and have a nice char.
While grilling, you can brush the pork belly with any remaining marinade for extra flavor.
Once the pork belly is grilled, transfer it to a serving plate.

Prepare a platter with lettuce leaves, ssamjang, kimchi, sliced garlic, sliced green onions, and cooked rice.
To eat, place a slice of grilled pork belly in a lettuce leaf, add a dollop of ssamjang, some kimchi, sliced garlic, and green onions. Optionally, add a bit of cooked rice.
Wrap the ingredients in the lettuce leaf and enjoy the Grilled Pork Belly Wrap.

Bossam is often served as a DIY dish, allowing each person to customize their wraps with their preferred condiments. It's a flavorful and interactive meal that's perfect for gatherings and family meals.

Gochujang Honey Glazed Salmon

Ingredients:

- 4 salmon fillets
- Salt and black pepper to taste
- 2 tablespoons gochujang (Korean red chili paste)
- 2 tablespoons honey
- 1 tablespoon soy sauce
- 1 tablespoon rice vinegar
- 1 tablespoon sesame oil
- 2 cloves garlic, minced
- 1 tablespoon grated ginger
- Sesame seeds and sliced green onions for garnish (optional)

Instructions:

Preheat your oven to 400°F (200°C).
Season the salmon fillets with salt and black pepper.
In a bowl, whisk together gochujang, honey, soy sauce, rice vinegar, sesame oil, minced garlic, and grated ginger to create the glaze.
Place the salmon fillets on a baking sheet lined with parchment paper.
Brush the salmon fillets generously with the gochujang honey glaze.
Bake in the preheated oven for about 12-15 minutes or until the salmon is cooked through and flakes easily with a fork.
While baking, you can brush the salmon with additional glaze halfway through the cooking time for extra flavor.
Once the salmon is cooked, remove it from the oven.
Optional: Drizzle any remaining glaze over the salmon for a glossy finish.
Garnish with sesame seeds and sliced green onions if desired.
Serve the Gochujang Honey Glazed Salmon hot, accompanied by your favorite side dishes or over a bed of rice.

Enjoy the perfect balance of sweet and spicy flavors in this Gochujang Honey Glazed Salmon. It's a quick and delicious way to elevate your salmon dish with a Korean-inspired twist.

Spicy Grilled Tofu

Ingredients:

- 1 block firm or extra-firm tofu, pressed and drained
- 2 tablespoons soy sauce
- 1 tablespoon sriracha or your favorite hot sauce
- 1 tablespoon maple syrup or agave nectar
- 1 tablespoon sesame oil
- 2 cloves garlic, minced
- 1 teaspoon grated ginger
- 1 tablespoon rice vinegar
- 1 tablespoon vegetable oil for grilling
- Sesame seeds and chopped green onions for garnish (optional)

Instructions:

Press the tofu to remove excess water. You can use a tofu press or wrap the tofu block in a clean kitchen towel, place it on a plate, and top it with a heavy object. Let it press for at least 15-20 minutes.
Once pressed, cut the tofu into slices or cubes, depending on your preference.
In a bowl, whisk together soy sauce, sriracha, maple syrup or agave nectar, sesame oil, minced garlic, grated ginger, and rice vinegar to create the marinade.
Place the tofu pieces in a shallow dish or a resealable plastic bag.
Pour the marinade over the tofu, ensuring each piece is well-coated. Marinate for at least 30 minutes to allow the flavors to infuse.
Preheat your grill or grill pan over medium-high heat.
Brush the grill grates with vegetable oil to prevent sticking.
Grill the marinated tofu for about 3-4 minutes on each side or until it has a nice char and is heated through.
While grilling, you can brush the tofu with any remaining marinade for extra flavor.
Once the tofu is grilled, transfer it to a serving plate.
Optional: Garnish with sesame seeds and chopped green onions.
Serve the Spicy Grilled Tofu hot, either on its own, in a salad, or as part of a stir-fry.

Enjoy the spicy kick and smoky flavor of this Spicy Grilled Tofu, perfect for a vegetarian or vegan meal option.

Korean BBQ Cauliflower Bites

Ingredients:

For the Cauliflower Bites:

- 1 medium-sized cauliflower, cut into florets
- 1 cup all-purpose flour
- 1 cup water
- 1 cup panko breadcrumbs
- Salt and pepper to taste
- Cooking spray or vegetable oil for baking

For the Korean BBQ Sauce:

- 1/4 cup soy sauce
- 2 tablespoons gochujang (Korean red chili paste)
- 2 tablespoons maple syrup or agave nectar
- 1 tablespoon rice vinegar
- 1 tablespoon sesame oil
- 2 cloves garlic, minced
- 1 teaspoon grated ginger
- Sesame seeds and chopped green onions for garnish (optional)

Instructions:

Preheat your oven to 425°F (220°C) and line a baking sheet with parchment paper.
In a bowl, whisk together flour and water to create a batter with a consistency similar to pancake batter.
Place panko breadcrumbs in a separate bowl.
Dip each cauliflower floret into the batter, allowing excess batter to drip off, and then coat it in panko breadcrumbs. Ensure the cauliflower is well-coated.
Place the coated cauliflower on the prepared baking sheet. Repeat for all cauliflower florets.
Lightly spray the cauliflower with cooking spray or drizzle with vegetable oil to help them crisp up during baking.
Bake in the preheated oven for about 20-25 minutes or until the cauliflower is golden brown and crispy.

While the cauliflower is baking, prepare the Korean BBQ sauce. In a small saucepan, combine soy sauce, gochujang, maple syrup or agave nectar, rice vinegar, sesame oil, minced garlic, and grated ginger. Simmer over low heat until the sauce thickens slightly.

Once the cauliflower bites are cooked, transfer them to a large bowl.

Pour the Korean BBQ sauce over the cauliflower bites and toss until they are evenly coated.

Optional: Garnish with sesame seeds and chopped green onions.

Serve the Korean BBQ Cauliflower Bites hot as a delicious appetizer or snack.

Enjoy the sweet, savory, and slightly spicy flavor of these Korean BBQ Cauliflower Bites, a tasty and creative way to incorporate cauliflower into your meals.

Grilled Portobello Mushrooms with Sesame Dressing

Ingredients:

For the Grilled Portobello Mushrooms:

- 4 large portobello mushrooms, stems removed
- 2 tablespoons olive oil
- Salt and black pepper to taste

For the Sesame Dressing:

- 3 tablespoons soy sauce
- 2 tablespoons rice vinegar
- 1 tablespoon sesame oil
- 1 tablespoon honey or maple syrup
- 1 clove garlic, minced
- 1 teaspoon grated ginger
- 1 tablespoon toasted sesame seeds
- Chopped green onions for garnish (optional)

Instructions:

Preheat your grill or grill pan over medium-high heat.
Clean the portobello mushrooms and remove the stems.
Brush both sides of the mushrooms with olive oil and season with salt and black pepper.
Grill the portobello mushrooms for about 4-5 minutes on each side, or until they are tender and have nice grill marks.
While the mushrooms are grilling, prepare the sesame dressing. In a bowl, whisk together soy sauce, rice vinegar, sesame oil, honey or maple syrup, minced garlic, grated ginger, and toasted sesame seeds.
Once the mushrooms are grilled, transfer them to a serving plate.
Drizzle the sesame dressing over the grilled portobello mushrooms.
Optional: Garnish with chopped green onions for added freshness.
Serve the Grilled Portobello Mushrooms with Sesame Dressing immediately as a delicious appetizer or side.

Enjoy the rich umami flavor of the grilled portobello mushrooms combined with the nutty and savory notes of the sesame dressing. This dish is not only tasty but also a great option for those looking for a vegetarian or vegan grilling option.

Grilled Sweet Potatoes with Soy Glaze

Ingredients:

- 2 large sweet potatoes, peeled and sliced into rounds
- 2 tablespoons vegetable oil
- Salt and black pepper to taste

For the Soy Glaze:

- 3 tablespoons soy sauce
- 2 tablespoons maple syrup or honey
- 1 tablespoon rice vinegar
- 1 teaspoon sesame oil
- 2 cloves garlic, minced
- 1 teaspoon grated ginger
- Sesame seeds and chopped green onions for garnish (optional)

Instructions:

Preheat your grill or grill pan over medium-high heat.
In a bowl, toss the sweet potato rounds with vegetable oil, salt, and black pepper.
Grill the sweet potato rounds for about 4-5 minutes on each side, or until they are tender and have nice grill marks.
While the sweet potatoes are grilling, prepare the soy glaze. In a small saucepan, combine soy sauce, maple syrup or honey, rice vinegar, sesame oil, minced garlic, and grated ginger. Simmer over low heat until the sauce thickens slightly.
Once the sweet potatoes are grilled, transfer them to a serving platter.
Drizzle the soy glaze over the grilled sweet potatoes.
Optional: Garnish with sesame seeds and chopped green onions for added flavor and freshness.
Serve the Grilled Sweet Potatoes with Soy Glaze hot as a delightful side dish.

Enjoy the combination of the smoky grilled flavor of sweet potatoes with the savory-sweet notes of the soy glaze. It's a tasty and nutritious addition to your barbecue or grilling menu.

Bulgogi Burritos

Ingredients:

For the Bulgogi Marinade:

- 1.5 to 2 pounds thinly sliced beef (ribeye or sirloin)
- 1/2 cup soy sauce
- 1/4 cup sugar
- 3 tablespoons mirin (rice wine) or cooking wine
- 2 tablespoons sesame oil
- 3 cloves garlic, minced
- 1 tablespoon grated ginger
- 2 green onions, chopped
- 1 tablespoon vegetable oil (for cooking)

For the Burritos:

- Flour tortillas
- Cooked white or brown rice
- Shredded lettuce
- Sliced avocado
- Sour cream or Greek yogurt
- Sliced cucumbers
- Kimchi (optional)
- Sesame seeds and chopped green onions for garnish

Instructions:

In a bowl, mix together soy sauce, sugar, mirin, sesame oil, minced garlic, grated ginger, and chopped green onions to create the bulgogi marinade.
Add the thinly sliced beef to the marinade, ensuring the meat is well-coated.
Marinate for at least 30 minutes to allow the flavors to infuse.
Heat vegetable oil in a skillet or wok over medium-high heat.
Stir-fry the marinated beef until it is cooked through and has a nice caramelized exterior. Remove from heat and set aside.
Assemble the burritos by placing a tortilla on a flat surface.
Add a layer of cooked rice in the center of the tortilla.
Top the rice with a portion of the cooked bulgogi.

Layer on shredded lettuce, sliced avocado, cucumber slices, and kimchi if desired.
Drizzle with sour cream or Greek yogurt.
Garnish with sesame seeds and chopped green onions.
Fold the sides of the tortilla over the filling and roll it up to form a burrito.
Repeat the process for the remaining burritos.
Serve the Bulgogi Burritos hot, either as is or with your favorite dipping sauce.

Enjoy the delicious fusion of Korean and Mexican flavors in these Bulgogi Burritos. They make for a hearty and satisfying meal, perfect for lunch or dinner.

Kimchi Quesadillas

Ingredients:

- Flour tortillas
- 1 cup shredded mozzarella cheese
- 1 cup shredded cheddar cheese
- 1 cup kimchi, drained and chopped
- 2 green onions, finely chopped
- 1 tablespoon sesame oil
- Sour cream or Greek yogurt for serving (optional)
- Sriracha or gochujang for extra spice (optional)

Instructions:

In a bowl, mix together the shredded mozzarella and cheddar cheeses.
Heat a non-stick skillet or griddle over medium heat.
Place a tortilla in the skillet and sprinkle a generous amount of the shredded cheese mixture over half of the tortilla.
Add a layer of chopped kimchi and sprinkle green onions on top of the cheese.
Drizzle a little sesame oil over the filling.
Fold the other half of the tortilla over the filling, creating a half-moon shape.
Press down gently with a spatula and cook for about 2-3 minutes on each side, or until the tortilla is golden brown and the cheese is melted.
Repeat the process for the remaining tortillas.
Once each quesadilla is cooked, remove it from the skillet and let it cool for a moment.
Optional: Cut the quesadillas into wedges.
Serve the Kimchi Quesadillas hot, with sour cream or Greek yogurt on the side for dipping.
For extra spice, drizzle Sriracha or gochujang over the quesadillas before serving.

Enjoy the unique and flavorful combination of kimchi and melted cheese in these Kimchi Quesadillas. They make for a tasty and creative snack or meal option.

Grilled Miso-Ginger Glazed Eggplant

Ingredients:

- 2 large Japanese or Chinese eggplants, sliced lengthwise
- 2 tablespoons miso paste (white or red miso)
- 2 tablespoons soy sauce
- 1 tablespoon rice vinegar
- 1 tablespoon mirin (rice wine) or dry sherry
- 1 tablespoon sesame oil
- 1 tablespoon grated ginger
- 2 cloves garlic, minced
- 1 tablespoon vegetable oil (for grilling)
- Sesame seeds and chopped green onions for garnish (optional)

Instructions:

Preheat your grill or grill pan over medium-high heat.
In a bowl, whisk together miso paste, soy sauce, rice vinegar, mirin, sesame oil, grated ginger, and minced garlic to create the miso-ginger glaze.
Slice the eggplants lengthwise, creating long strips.
Brush each side of the eggplant slices with vegetable oil to prevent sticking on the grill.
Grill the eggplant slices for about 2-3 minutes on each side or until they are tender and have nice grill marks.
During the last minute of grilling, brush the miso-ginger glaze over each side of the eggplant, allowing it to caramelize slightly.
Once the eggplant is grilled and glazed, transfer the slices to a serving plate.
Optional: Sprinkle sesame seeds and chopped green onions on top for garnish.
Serve the Grilled Miso-Ginger Glazed Eggplant hot as a side dish or appetizer.

Enjoy the rich umami flavors of the miso-ginger glaze paired with the smokiness of grilled eggplant. This dish makes for a delicious and elegant addition to your summer grilling menu.

Soy Sesame Grilled Scallops

Ingredients:

- 1 pound fresh scallops, patted dry
- 2 tablespoons soy sauce
- 1 tablespoon sesame oil
- 1 tablespoon rice vinegar
- 1 tablespoon honey or maple syrup
- 2 cloves garlic, minced
- 1 teaspoon grated ginger
- Sesame seeds and chopped green onions for garnish (optional)
- Lemon wedges for serving

Instructions:

In a bowl, whisk together soy sauce, sesame oil, rice vinegar, honey or maple syrup, minced garlic, and grated ginger to create the marinade.
Place the fresh scallops in a shallow dish or a resealable plastic bag.
Pour the marinade over the scallops, ensuring each scallop is well-coated.
Marinate for at least 15-20 minutes.
Preheat your grill or grill pan over medium-high heat.
Thread the scallops onto skewers if you prefer for easy grilling.
Grill the scallops for about 2-3 minutes on each side or until they are opaque and have grill marks.
While grilling, you can brush the scallops with any remaining marinade for extra flavor.
Once the scallops are grilled, transfer them to a serving plate.
Optional: Sprinkle sesame seeds and chopped green onions on top for garnish.
Serve the Soy Sesame Grilled Scallops hot, with lemon wedges on the side.

Enjoy the succulent and flavorful Soy Sesame Grilled Scallops as a delightful appetizer or as part of a seafood feast. The combination of soy sauce, sesame, and honey adds a perfect balance of savory and sweet notes to the scallops.

Gochujang Glazed Brussels Sprouts

Ingredients:

- 1 pound Brussels sprouts, trimmed and halved
- 2 tablespoons vegetable oil
- Salt and black pepper to taste

For the Gochujang Glaze:

- 2 tablespoons gochujang (Korean red chili paste)
- 2 tablespoons soy sauce
- 1 tablespoon maple syrup or honey
- 1 tablespoon rice vinegar
- 1 tablespoon sesame oil
- 2 cloves garlic, minced
- Sesame seeds and chopped green onions for garnish (optional)

Instructions:

Preheat your oven to 400°F (200°C).
In a bowl, toss the halved Brussels sprouts with vegetable oil, salt, and black pepper.
Spread the Brussels sprouts in a single layer on a baking sheet lined with parchment paper.
Roast in the preheated oven for about 20-25 minutes or until the Brussels sprouts are golden brown and crispy on the edges.
While the Brussels sprouts are roasting, prepare the gochujang glaze. In a small saucepan, combine gochujang, soy sauce, maple syrup or honey, rice vinegar, sesame oil, and minced garlic. Simmer over low heat until the glaze thickens slightly.
Once the Brussels sprouts are roasted, transfer them to a bowl.
Pour the gochujang glaze over the roasted Brussels sprouts and toss until they are evenly coated.
Optional: Garnish with sesame seeds and chopped green onions for added flavor.
Serve the Gochujang Glazed Brussels Sprouts hot as a delicious side dish.

Enjoy the bold and spicy flavors of gochujang paired with the crispy texture of roasted Brussels sprouts. This dish makes for a flavorful and unique addition to your vegetable side dish repertoire.

Bulgogi Lettuce Cup Tacos

Ingredients:

For the Bulgogi Marinade:

- 1.5 to 2 pounds thinly sliced beef (ribeye or sirloin)
- 1/2 cup soy sauce
- 1/4 cup sugar
- 3 tablespoons mirin (rice wine) or cooking wine
- 2 tablespoons sesame oil
- 3 cloves garlic, minced
- 1 tablespoon grated ginger
- 2 green onions, chopped
- 1 tablespoon vegetable oil (for cooking)

For the Lettuce Cup Tacos:

- Butter or iceberg lettuce leaves, washed and separated
- Cooked white or brown rice
- Shredded carrots
- Sliced cucumbers
- Kimchi
- Sesame seeds and chopped green onions for garnish (optional)

Instructions:

In a bowl, mix together soy sauce, sugar, mirin, sesame oil, minced garlic, grated ginger, and chopped green onions to create the bulgogi marinade.
Add the thinly sliced beef to the marinade, ensuring the meat is well-coated.
Marinate for at least 30 minutes to allow the flavors to infuse.
Heat vegetable oil in a skillet or wok over medium-high heat.
Stir-fry the marinated beef until it is cooked through and has a nice caramelized exterior. Remove from heat and set aside.
Assemble the Lettuce Cup Tacos by placing a lettuce leaf on a flat surface.
Add a spoonful of cooked rice in the center of the lettuce leaf.
Top the rice with a portion of the cooked bulgogi.

Add shredded carrots, sliced cucumbers, and kimchi on top of the bulgogi.
Optional: Sprinkle sesame seeds and chopped green onions on top for garnish.
Fold the sides of the lettuce leaf over the filling to form a taco-like shape.
Repeat the process for the remaining Lettuce Cup Tacos.
Serve the Bulgogi Lettuce Cup Tacos hot, with additional kimchi on the side if desired.

Enjoy the unique combination of Korean bulgogi flavors and the refreshing crunch of lettuce in these delicious Lettuce Cup Tacos. They make for a light and flavorful meal or appetizer.

Grilled Pineapple with Honey-Soy Glaze

Ingredients:

- 1 whole pineapple, peeled, cored, and cut into rings or wedges
- 1/4 cup honey
- 2 tablespoons soy sauce
- 1 tablespoon melted butter or coconut oil
- 1 teaspoon grated ginger
- Optional: Vanilla ice cream or Greek yogurt for serving
- Optional: Mint leaves for garnish

Instructions:

Preheat your grill or grill pan over medium-high heat.
In a bowl, whisk together honey, soy sauce, melted butter or coconut oil, and grated ginger to create the glaze.
Brush the pineapple rings or wedges with the honey-soy glaze, ensuring they are well-coated on all sides.
Place the glazed pineapple on the preheated grill.
Grill the pineapple for about 2-3 minutes on each side or until it has nice grill marks and is slightly caramelized.
While grilling, you can brush the pineapple with any remaining glaze for extra flavor.
Once the pineapple is grilled, transfer it to a serving plate.
Optional: Serve the Grilled Pineapple with a scoop of vanilla ice cream or a dollop of Greek yogurt.
Optional: Garnish with mint leaves for a fresh touch.
Serve the Grilled Pineapple with Honey-Soy Glaze warm and enjoy!

This dish is a delightful blend of sweetness from the honey, the savory depth from soy sauce, and the caramelized goodness from grilling. It's a simple and elegant dessert or side that's sure to please your taste buds.

Bulgogi Sliders

Ingredients:

For the Bulgogi Marinade:

- 1.5 to 2 pounds thinly sliced beef (ribeye or sirloin)
- 1/2 cup soy sauce
- 1/4 cup sugar
- 3 tablespoons mirin (rice wine) or cooking wine
- 2 tablespoons sesame oil
- 3 cloves garlic, minced
- 1 tablespoon grated ginger
- 2 green onions, chopped
- 1 tablespoon vegetable oil (for cooking)

For the Sliders:

- Mini slider buns or dinner rolls
- Sliced cheese (your choice, such as provolone or cheddar)
- Lettuce leaves
- Sliced tomatoes
- Mayonnaise or your favorite sauce

Instructions:

In a bowl, mix together soy sauce, sugar, mirin, sesame oil, minced garlic, grated ginger, and chopped green onions to create the bulgogi marinade.
Add the thinly sliced beef to the marinade, ensuring the meat is well-coated.
Marinate for at least 30 minutes to allow the flavors to infuse.
Heat vegetable oil in a skillet or wok over medium-high heat.
Stir-fry the marinated beef until it is cooked through and has a nice caramelized exterior. Remove from heat and set aside.
Toast the mini slider buns or dinner rolls in the oven or on a skillet.
Assemble the Bulgogi Sliders by placing a lettuce leaf on the bottom half of each bun.
Top the lettuce with a portion of the cooked bulgogi.

Add a slice of cheese on top of the bulgogi.
Place a slice of tomato on the cheese.
Spread mayonnaise or your favorite sauce on the top half of the bun.
Sandwich the sliders together.
Repeat the process for the remaining sliders.
Serve the Bulgogi Sliders hot and enjoy!

These Bulgogi Sliders are not only delicious but also a great way to showcase the rich and savory flavors of Korean bulgogi in a convenient and shareable format. Perfect for gatherings or as a unique addition to your appetizer menu.

Spicy Grilled Avocado

Ingredients:

- 2 ripe avocados, halved and pitted
- 2 tablespoons olive oil
- 1 tablespoon lime juice
- 1 teaspoon chili powder
- 1/2 teaspoon cayenne pepper (adjust to taste)
- Salt and black pepper to taste
- Fresh cilantro for garnish (optional)

Instructions:

Preheat your grill or grill pan over medium-high heat.
In a bowl, whisk together olive oil, lime juice, chili powder, cayenne pepper, salt, and black pepper.
Brush the cut sides of the avocado halves with the spicy olive oil mixture.
Place the avocado halves on the preheated grill, cut side down.
Grill for about 2-3 minutes or until the avocados have grill marks and are slightly charred.
Carefully flip the avocados with a spatula and grill for an additional 1-2 minutes.
Remove the grilled avocados from the heat and place them on a serving plate.
Optional: Drizzle any remaining spicy olive oil mixture over the grilled avocados.
Garnish with fresh cilantro if desired.
Serve the Spicy Grilled Avocado immediately as a side dish or a unique appetizer.

Enjoy the warm, smoky flavor of the grilled avocados with a spicy twist. This dish is not only delicious but also adds a creative touch to your grilling repertoire.

Grilled Korean Egg Toast

Ingredients:

- 4 slices of bread (white or whole wheat)
- 4 eggs
- 1/4 cup milk
- Salt and black pepper to taste
- 2 tablespoons unsalted butter
- 1 small carrot, julienned
- 1/2 small onion, thinly sliced
- 1/4 cup bell peppers, thinly sliced (red or green)
- 4 slices of ham or bacon (optional)
- Ketchup or mayonnaise for drizzling (optional)
- Fresh parsley or chives for garnish (optional)

Instructions:

In a bowl, whisk together the eggs, milk, salt, and black pepper until well combined.
Heat a non-stick skillet or griddle over medium heat and melt 1 tablespoon of butter.
Dip each slice of bread into the egg mixture, ensuring both sides are well-coated.
Place the coated bread slices on the skillet and cook until the bottom is golden brown.
Flip the bread slices and cook the other side until golden brown and the eggs are fully cooked.
Remove the egg-coated bread from the skillet and set aside.
In the same skillet, add the remaining tablespoon of butter.
Add the julienned carrot, sliced onion, and bell peppers. Sauté until the vegetables are softened.
If using ham or bacon, cook them in the skillet until they are done.
Assemble the Grilled Korean Egg Toast by placing the cooked vegetables on a slice of egg-coated bread.
Add a slice of ham or bacon on top (if using).
Top with another slice of egg-coated bread.
Optional: Drizzle with ketchup or mayonnaise for added flavor.
Repeat the process for the remaining slices.

Garnish with fresh parsley or chives if desired.
Serve the Grilled Korean Egg Toast hot and enjoy!

This delicious and satisfying Korean street food is a delightful way to enjoy a flavorful and filling breakfast or brunch.

Korean BBQ Meat Skewers

Ingredients:

For the Marinade:

- 1.5 to 2 pounds of your choice of meat (beef, chicken, pork), cut into bite-sized pieces
- 1/4 cup soy sauce
- 2 tablespoons mirin (rice wine) or dry sherry
- 2 tablespoons sesame oil
- 1 tablespoon sugar
- 3 cloves garlic, minced
- 1 teaspoon grated ginger
- 1 tablespoon sesame seeds
- 2 green onions, chopped
- Wooden skewers, soaked in water for at least 30 minutes

For Dipping Sauce (Optional):

- 1/4 cup soy sauce
- 1 tablespoon rice vinegar
- 1 teaspoon sesame oil
- 1 teaspoon sugar
- 1 teaspoon sesame seeds
- Chopped green onions for garnish

Instructions:

In a bowl, combine soy sauce, mirin, sesame oil, sugar, minced garlic, grated ginger, sesame seeds, and chopped green onions to create the marinade.
Place the bite-sized meat pieces in the marinade, ensuring each piece is well-coated. Marinate for at least 1-2 hours or overnight for maximum flavor.
Preheat your grill or grill pan over medium-high heat.
Thread the marinated meat onto the soaked wooden skewers.
Grill the meat skewers for about 8-10 minutes, turning occasionally, until the meat is fully cooked and has a nice char on the edges.

While grilling, you can baste the skewers with any remaining marinade for extra flavor.
Optional: In a small bowl, mix together soy sauce, rice vinegar, sesame oil, sugar, and sesame seeds to create a dipping sauce.
Once the meat skewers are cooked, transfer them to a serving plate.
Optional: Garnish with chopped green onions.
Serve the Korean BBQ Meat Skewers hot, with the optional dipping sauce on the side.

Enjoy these flavorful and tender Korean BBQ Meat Skewers as a delightful appetizer or part of a larger Korean BBQ feast. The marinade imparts a perfect blend of savory, sweet, and smoky flavors to the meat.

Bulgogi-stuffed Bell Peppers

Ingredients:

For the Bulgogi Marinade:

- 1.5 to 2 pounds thinly sliced beef (ribeye or sirloin)
- 1/2 cup soy sauce
- 1/4 cup sugar
- 3 tablespoons mirin (rice wine) or cooking wine
- 2 tablespoons sesame oil
- 3 cloves garlic, minced
- 1 tablespoon grated ginger
- 2 green onions, chopped
- 1 tablespoon vegetable oil (for cooking)

For the Stuffed Bell Peppers:

- 4 large bell peppers, halved and seeds removed
- 1 cup cooked white or brown rice
- Bulgogi marinade (reserved from above)
- 1 cup shredded cheese (cheddar or mozzarella)
- Sesame seeds and chopped green onions for garnish (optional)

Instructions:

Preheat your oven to 375°F (190°C).
In a bowl, mix together soy sauce, sugar, mirin, sesame oil, minced garlic, grated ginger, and chopped green onions to create the bulgogi marinade.
Add the thinly sliced beef to the marinade, ensuring the meat is well-coated.
Marinate for at least 30 minutes to allow the flavors to infuse.
Heat vegetable oil in a skillet or wok over medium-high heat.
Stir-fry the marinated beef until it is cooked through and has a nice caramelized exterior. Remove from heat and set aside.
In a large mixing bowl, combine the cooked rice, cooked bulgogi, and half of the shredded cheese. Mix well.
Place the bell pepper halves in a baking dish.

Stuff each bell pepper half with the rice and bulgogi mixture.
Top each stuffed pepper with the remaining shredded cheese.
Bake in the preheated oven for about 20-25 minutes or until the bell peppers are tender and the cheese is melted and bubbly.
Optional: Garnish with sesame seeds and chopped green onions.
Serve the Bulgogi-stuffed Bell Peppers hot as a delicious and wholesome main dish.

Enjoy the combination of the sweet and savory bulgogi filling with the vibrant and tender bell peppers. This dish is not only visually appealing but also a flavorful twist on traditional stuffed peppers.

Grilled Kimchi Stuffed Mushrooms

Ingredients:

- 16 large white or cremini mushrooms, cleaned and stems removed
- 1 cup kimchi, finely chopped
- 1/2 cup cream cheese, softened
- 2 tablespoons soy sauce
- 1 tablespoon sesame oil
- 1 tablespoon green onions, finely chopped
- 1 teaspoon sugar (optional)
- Sesame seeds and additional green onions for garnish (optional)

Instructions:

Preheat your grill or grill pan over medium-high heat.
In a bowl, mix together chopped kimchi, softened cream cheese, soy sauce, sesame oil, green onions, and sugar (if using).
Stuff each mushroom cap with the kimchi and cream cheese mixture.
Place the stuffed mushrooms on the preheated grill.
Grill for about 10-12 minutes or until the mushrooms are tender and have nice grill marks.
Optional: During grilling, you can baste the mushrooms with any remaining kimchi and cream cheese mixture for extra flavor.
Once the mushrooms are grilled, transfer them to a serving plate.
Optional: Garnish with sesame seeds and additional chopped green onions.
Serve the Grilled Kimchi Stuffed Mushrooms hot as a flavorful and unique appetizer.

Enjoy the savory, spicy, and creamy combination of grilled mushrooms and kimchi. These stuffed mushrooms make for a delicious addition to any barbecue or party menu, offering a delightful twist on traditional stuffed mushrooms.

Korean BBQ Chicken Pizza

Ingredients:

For the Korean BBQ Chicken:

- 1 pound boneless, skinless chicken breasts, thinly sliced
- 1/2 cup Korean BBQ sauce (store-bought or homemade)
- 2 tablespoons soy sauce
- 1 tablespoon sesame oil
- 2 cloves garlic, minced
- 1 tablespoon sugar
- 1 teaspoon grated ginger

For the Pizza:

- 1 pizza dough (store-bought or homemade)
- 1 cup shredded mozzarella cheese
- 1 cup shredded cooked chicken (from the Korean BBQ Chicken)
- 1/2 cup sliced red bell pepper
- 1/2 cup sliced red onion
- 1/4 cup chopped green onions
- Sesame seeds for garnish
- Optional: Drizzle of additional Korean BBQ sauce for extra flavor

Instructions:

Preheat your oven to the temperature recommended for your pizza dough.
In a bowl, mix together the sliced chicken with Korean BBQ sauce, soy sauce, sesame oil, minced garlic, sugar, and grated ginger. Let it marinate for at least 15-30 minutes.
In a skillet over medium-high heat, cook the marinated chicken until fully cooked and caramelized. Set aside.
Roll out the pizza dough on a lightly floured surface to your desired thickness.
Transfer the rolled-out dough to a pizza stone or a baking sheet lined with parchment paper.
Spread a thin layer of Korean BBQ sauce over the pizza dough.
Sprinkle shredded mozzarella cheese evenly over the sauce.

Distribute the cooked Korean BBQ chicken, sliced red bell pepper, and sliced red onion over the cheese.

Bake in the preheated oven according to the pizza dough instructions or until the crust is golden and the cheese is melted and bubbly.

Once out of the oven, sprinkle chopped green onions and sesame seeds over the pizza.

Optional: Drizzle additional Korean BBQ sauce over the top for extra flavor.

Slice and serve the Korean BBQ Chicken Pizza hot.

Enjoy the unique fusion of Korean barbecue and pizza in this delicious and flavorful dish. It's a crowd-pleaser that brings together the best of both worlds.

www.ingramcontent.com/pod-product-compliance
Lightning Source LLC
LaVergne TN
LVHW081613060526
838201LV00054B/2229